SIZZLI Celeb

Logan!

RISING STAR LOGAN LERMAN

★

BY STEPHEN ELDRIDGE

Enslow Publishers, Inc.
40 Industrial Road
Box 398
Berkeley Heights, NJ 07922
USA

http://www.enslow.com

Copyright © 2014 by Enslow Publishers, Inc.

Library of Congress Cataloging-in-Publication Data:

Eldridge, Stephen.
  Logan! : rising star Logan Lerman / by Stephen Eldridge.
     pages cm. — (Sizzling celebrities)
  Includes index.
  Summary: "Read about Logan's early life, how he got started in acting, and his future plans"—Provided by publisher.
  ISBN 978-0-7660-4171-4
  1. Lerman, Logan, 1992- —Juvenile literature. 2. Actors—United States—Biography—Juvenile literature. I. Title.
PN2287.L4325E43 2014
791.4302'8092—dc23
  [B]

                                                    2012040317

Future editions:
Paperback ISBN: 978-1-4644-0281-4
EPUB ISBN: 978-1-4645-1177-6
Single-User PDF ISBN: 978-1-4646-1177-3
Multi-User PDF ISBN: 978-0-7660-5806-4

Printed in China

012013 Leo Paper Group, Heshan City, Guangdong, China

10 9 8 7 6 5 4 3 2 1

To Our Readers: We have done our best to make sure all Internet addresses in this book were active and appropriate when we went to press. However, the author and the publisher have no control over and assume no liability for the material available on those Internet sites or on other Web sites they may link to. Any comments or suggestions can be sent by e-mail to comments@enslow.com or to the address on the back cover.

Illustration Credits: AP Photo, p. 17; AP Photo: Charles Sykes, pp. 7, 24, 37, 40, Dan Steinberg, p. 29, Danny Moloshok, p. 2, 19, Elise Amendola, p. 11, Itsuo Inouye, p. 44, Jim Cooper, p. 13, Joel Ryan, pp. 1, 4, 43, Matt Sayles, pp. 15, 22, 27, Peter Kramer, p. 32, Rene Macura, p. 25, Richard Drew, p. 8, Starpix, Dale Alocca, 39; Chris Pizzello/Invision/AP, p. 46.

Cover Photo: AP Photo/ Joel Ryan

Contents

Not Born a Hero

Fire bursts from the jaws of a monster. The creature has five heads, each filled with razor-sharp teeth. It towers over a teenager and spews flame at him. Only a bronze shield on the boy's arm protects him. He runs and dives behind a marble statue. The monster chases him, continuing to breathe fire. The shield grows too hot to hold, and the boy drops it. Defenseless, he looks around for something that can save his life. What he sees is a water fountain. For a normal teenager, this would be useless. But this teenager is Percy Jackson, the son of the sea god Poseidon, and for him water is a weapon. He reaches out toward the fountain and it bursts from the wall. Water gushes out and surrounds the monster, saving the young hero's life.

This is a scene from the movie *Percy Jackson & The Olympians: The Lightning Thief*. But in real life, the monster is a computer-generated image. The shield is a prop. And Percy Jackson isn't the son of a god, but Logan Lerman, an actor with a talent for playing young heroes.

◀ *Logan Lerman starred in* Percy Jackson & The Olympians: The Lightning Thief, *an exciting film filled with action and adventure. Here he his at the premiere for the film.*

The Actor Behind the Hero

Logan knows how easy it can be for an actor to mistakenly play himself rather than the character. When creating the role of Percy, Lerman worked with his director, Chris Columbus. They wanted to make it clear that the young actor wasn't just playing himself. "I wanted to make sure that it's a character," he told Jenny Cooney, for girl.com. "And I gave him this Brooklyn accent, changing the way he walks or very subtle characteristics so that I could separate myself from the character."

Unlike Percy Jackson, Logan Lerman isn't a New Yorker. He was born and raised thousands of miles away in Beverly Hills, California. His father wasn't Poseidon, of course. In fact, you could say the Lerman family helps with the work of another Greek god—Apollo, the god associated with healing. Lerman's family owns Lerman and Son, a company that sells medical equipment. Logan's father, Lawrence, specializes in medical tools that help children.

The Lerman family has run the company for nearly a hundred years. Logan's great-grandfather, Jacob Lerman, started the company in Germany. However, the Lerman family was forced to flee the country due to the rise of the Nazis. The Nazis were a political party that hated Jewish families like the Lermans. After spending about a decade in Shanghai, China, the family moved to California, where their business thrived.

Logan made the character of Percy Jackson have a Brooklyn, New York accent. The actor had a chance to visit the Empire State Building, also in New York

While Percy grows up without knowing most of his family, Logan has a brother, Lucas, and a sister, Lindsey. The family still lives together in their California home. One thing Logan and Percy have in common, though, is an important relationship with their mothers. Lisa Lerman was the first person Logan told he wanted to be an actor. She helped Logan get his first roles and has acted as her son's manager since he was a small child. Since Logan was young, they have traveled the country together for Logan's work.

Born to Make Movies

Movies have been important to Logan for almost his entire life. Logan was born on January 19, 1992. Growing up in Beverly Hills meant Logan was close to Hollywood. He says he was in the "right place at the right time" to get into acting. The story goes that as a two-year-old toddler, Logan

◄ *Logan loved watching the movies of Chinese martial artist Jackie Chan.*

watched a movie starring martial artist Jackie Chan. After the film, he told his mother he wanted to be an actor. Lisa took her young son's desire to act seriously and helped him begin his career. He was signed by a talent agent when he was just four years old.

When he was very young, Logan didn't plan on acting as a career. In an interview with the Irish Web site RTÉ he said, "I started when I was really young . . . but that was just to do something to get out of school." Nevertheless, he soon began acting in commercials. This helped him earn membership in the Screen Actors Guild. The Screen Actors Guild is a group that represents actors and helps to set rules for how they work and are paid. When Logan became a member, it gave him many more career opportunities.

Logan grew up as a normal kid in many ways. However, from an early age he had to balance his regular life with show business. Just a few short years after he told his mother he wanted to be an actor, he would be appearing in major motion pictures.

2 Breaking Into Movies

Logan's film debut came in director Roland Emmerich's *The Patriot*, starring Mel Gibson. *The Patriot* is historical fiction set during the American Revolution. The film tells the story of a man named Benjamin Martin (Gibson). At first, Martin doesn't take sides in the war. However, when British soldiers kill one of his sons, he decides to join the revolution and fight to help free the colonists. Logan plays Martin's youngest son, William Martin. The film also stars Heath Ledger as Gabriel Martin, Benjamin Martin's eldest son. It also features Jason Isaacs as the brutal British colonel, William Tavington.

Making Movies

Logan got another chance to work with Gibson in his very next film. *What Women Want*, from director Nancy Meyers, was released in 2000, the same year as *The Patriot*. Gibson plays Nick Marshall, a self-centered advertising executive. Marshall's life changes when a bizarre accident gives him the power to hear what women are thinking. At first he uses this power for his own benefit. However, a developing relationship with Darcy Maguire, played by Helen Hunt, changes his plans. This time, Logan plays a younger version of Mel Gibson's character. Though reviews for the film were mixed, it was an enormous success at the box office. It made more than $180 million in the United States alone.

Logan's next film role came in 2001, in Penny Marshall's *Riding in Cars with Boys*. Based on a true story, *Riding in Cars with Boys* stars Drew Barrymore. Barrymore plays Beverly Donofrio, a young mother and would-be writer. The film is set across several years, and Logan plays the eight-year-old version of Beverly's son, Jason. Then, in 2004, Logan appeared in the science-fiction thriller *The Butterfly Effect*. The film focuses on a young man named Evan (played by Ashton Kutcher) who discovers that he has the ability to travel

Logan plays a younger version of Drew Barrymore's character's son in Riding in Cars with Boys. *Here, Barrymore accepts the Woman of the Year Award from Harvard University's Hasty Pudding Theatricals in 2001.*

through time—with unpredictable results. Directed by Eric Bress and J. Mackye Gruber, the film also stars Amy Smart and Eric Stoltz. Logan plays the seven-year-old version of Evan.

Logan's career was off to a promising start. His work in these movies had proven that he was a talented young actor. However, his first starring role didn't come on a movie screen. Television would play an important role in his budding career.

Stepping Into the Spotlight

Logan first caught the attention of many critics in a made-for-TV movie based on a John Grisham novel. *A Painted House* aired on CBS in 2003. In his first starring role, Logan plays Luke Chandler, a 10-year-old boy growing up on a farm in Arkansas. Set in the 1950s, the film focuses on Luke's coming of age as he witnesses a murder, falls in love, and encounters classism and racism. Michael Speier of *Variety* praised Logan's performance, saying he was "strong as a precocious youngster around whom the entire story orbits."

In addition to critical praise, Logan's role in *A Painted House* won him his first Young Artist Award. The Young Artist Awards are given to artists under the age of eighteen in television, motion pictures, theater, and music. The awards also serve to provide scholarships for physically or financially challenged young people who want to work in the arts. Logan and actor Calum Worthy tied in the category of Best Performance in a TV Movie, Miniseries or Special for a Leading Young Actor.

From Hobby to Career

Believe it or not, Logan Lerman's career as an actor almost ended before it had really begun. Before Logan even had a chance to play Percy Jackson, he decided to retire from acting.

At age ten, Logan had never really taken acting seriously as a career. He viewed it more as something fun to do instead of schoolwork. Unfortunately, sometimes acting wasn't as much fun as he wanted it to be. "I didn't have a good experience," Logan said about his first acting jobs. "[I] just wanted to relax and go to school."

▲ *John Grisham wrote the novel* A Painted House, *which would be made into a movie that Logan Lerman would star in.*

Logan didn't act for about a year. But when he was twelve years old, two things brought him back to Hollywood. The first was his interest in film. According to Logan, when he first started acting he "didn't have any conscious awareness of what I was doing or what was going on." It was only after he took some time off that he began to develop his love of film and everything that goes into the filmmaking process. He told RTÉ, "… I got back into it again, to understand production, to be on set and understand filmmaking. It was just a hobby then it turned into a profession because I became more passionate about it and fell in love with each medium of filmmaking—acting being one of them."

For Logan, acting is a way to learn about the complicated world of filmmaking. When he was just starting out, he didn't understand how films were made. He says, "I had no concept of editing … I didn't understand anything; about how a camera worked or how to make films and that's when I opened my eyes and started learning more. It's been my life ever since."

Logan is inspired by actors who've transitioned into making their own films as directors. Since his decision to pursue acting as a career, he's started to write and come up with ideas for films. His interest in music is also a part of his passion for film. He told the magazine *Da Man*, "… I guess music was one of the first things I noticed early on. I noticed how it could affect the tone, or mood of the film."

While Logan doesn't think he's ready to step behind the camera and direct his own films yet, he's always learning. He says he'd have even loved to go to film school, but the opportunity to learn on actual film sets was too good to pass up. "[I]t's an opportunity to learn about film that few get: If you open your eyes and ask questions, one can really take advantage of it and make it the best educational experience that money could never have bought."

However, Logan may never have started on this path and discovered his passion for filmmaking without one more thing: a television show called *Jack & Bobby*.

▲ *Logan Lerman not only enjoys acting, but also the filmmaking process.*

The Boy Who Would Be President

Bobby McCallister is a young boy who doesn't fit in. Jack McCallister is his older, more popular brother. One day, one of them will be president of the United States, and will inspire Americans, many of whom will call him "the Great Believer." But today, they're just two kids struggling to live their lives.

Viewers didn't know which brother would be president when *Jack & Bobby* began airing on the WB in September 2004. Neither, of course, did the characters of Jack and Bobby. The show told the story of the McCallister presidency in the style of a documentary. Interviews and clips from the year 2049 told what the president's friends, family, allies, and enemies thought of him. Mainly, though, the show was set in the present day, with the characters unaware of the destinies that awaited them.

The Future Leader of the Free World

Jack & Bobby started as a simple idea—to show the childhood of a boy who would one day be president. The show was created by Greg Berlanti, Steve A. Cohen, Vanessa Taylor, and Brad Meltzer. Cohen and Meltzer collaborated together on the idea that would become *Jack & Bobby*. Cohen had worked with President Bill Clinton's press team and was very familiar with politics and politicians. Meltzer was a novelist and comic book writer. The two writers wanted to create a show

▼ *The first names of the title characters of Jack & Bobby are meant to remind Americans of President John F. Kennedy (left), who was killed in 1963, and his brother Robert F. Kennedy, who was his attorney general.*

that returned to the idea that anyone can grow up to be the president. Though the show lasted only one season both critics and fans loved it.

Logan plays Bobby, the younger of the two boys—the brother who will, about forty years later, become the inspirational President Robert McCallister. Logan portrays Bobby as a sensitive, socially awkward boy who has no idea he will one day become a great man. His brother, Jack, is played by Matt Long. Jack is a good-looking athlete with a rocky relationship with their mother, Grace. Grace, played by Christine Lahti, is a single mother and college professor with strong political beliefs. The show tells the story of how Grace and Jack influence Bobby and the leader he will become. The show often connected events in the family's lives to stories about the future McCallister presidency.

Perhaps where *Jack & Bobby* shined most brightly was its portrayal of how difficult it can be to be different as a teenager. As Gillian Flynn of *Entertainment Weekly* put it, the show "nails the perverse, political world of high school, where conformist kids are paid off with popularity and engaged oddballs like Bobby end up at lunch tables alone." The character of Jack puts it a different way in the first episode of the show: "Normal is what you have to be if you don't want to spend every day of high school getting beat up." However, while it's never easy for Bobby to be different, it's his differences that make him a success in the future.

For Logan Lerman, Bobby McCallister was the first in a long line of characters who couldn't fit in—but had a deep-down decency that made them heroes and leaders anyway. Like Bobby, Logan sometimes felt that he was a geek—a film geek, in his case: "... but I took that and I made it my strength."

▼ *In 2004, Logan Lerman (center) and his Jack & Bobby costar Matthew Long accept the Family Television Award for "best siblings."*

Gaining the World's Attention

Jack & Bobby was known for being a smart, well-written show with a great leading cast. Christine Lahti in particular stood out to critics—she was nominated both for a Golden Globe and for a Screen Actors Guild award. Matt and Logan's work was also highly praised. Robert Bianco of *USA Today* called Lahti's acting "almost breathtaking," but added "Lerman and Long keep up with her every step of the way." Logan also received another Young Artist Award for his work on the show. He won the award for the Best Performance in a TV Series (Comedy or Drama) by a leading young actor. He tied again, this time with Jack De Sena of the *Nickelodeon* show *All That*.

Although Logan had received praise from critics before, he now began to attract fans—including girls. At age twelve, most of Logan's friends were girls, but he didn't have a girlfriend. He was getting old enough to appreciate attention from female fans, though, and he'd begun to receive letters from them. Luckily, the letters did not go to his head. Logan still describes himself as "on the shy side."

"The Best Learning Experience"

Jack & Bobby had a very devoted audience that loved it, but unfortunately that group of fans wasn't very big. Despite stellar reviews, the show was canceled after its first season. Although *Jack & Bobby* lasted only a year, in many ways it helped to shape Logan's future career. Logan called it "just the best learning experience."

Logan talked to Michael Ordona of the *LA Times* about how the show put his career back on track. Although he'd acted from an early age, it was *Jack & Bobby* that helped him fall in love with the art of making movies. "That's when I started taking things seriously and I grew a major passion for filmmaking," he said. After doing the show, he became a serious film fan. He would go to the movies all the time, and he liked to catch up on classic films. Talking about his love of film, he said, ". . . discovering these great pieces of art; it fueled my passion for being in this business. It's really all I do with my life; I see movies."

Working on *Jack & Bobby* also introduced Logan to Dean Collins, another young actor with a passion for film. Dean played Warren Feide, Bobby's best friend. In a case of life imitating art, Logan and Dean quickly became good friends as well. The two were interested in film and the filmmaking process. They even shared an interest in music, and put together a band called Indigo. Though Logan called the band "just kind of a joke," several songs are available to stream on Myspace. The two had more serious plans for collaborating as well.

Together, the boys not only watched and studied movies, but also began creating them. In 2006, they began posting short videos on YouTube. The two friends posted their first short, "What Else Could Go Wrong" on September 4, 2006. The video is a four-minute comedy about a young man, played by Logan, who's having a very bad day. The duo's first video has

21

▲ Jack & Bobby *was a great learning experience for Logan Lerman.*

now gotten more than four hundred thousand views and more than four thousand "likes" on YouTube. Over the next five years, another nine videos by Logan, Dean, or both appeared. At one point, the two friends even considered making a feature-length film together. Unfortunately for fans of their videos, that project has yet to see the light of day.

The End of the Beginning

When *Jack & Bobby* went off the air, fans were crushed. However there was still a bright career ahead for Logan. Working on the show had helped him discover a love for the process of making films. It had also helped show his talent as an actor to the world. With a new focus on his study of movies as an art form, Logan returned to the world of feature films.

4 Becoming a Star

By the time he was thirteen, Logan had proven he could handle starring roles on television. After *Jack & Bobby* ended, he was ready to show the world he could take on a leading role in a feature film. He got his chance in the film *Hoot*. *Hoot* is directed by Wil Shriner and based on the novel by Carl Hiassen. When the film was released in 2006, Logan could finally say he'd starred in a Hollywood movie.

Carl Hiassen was already a successful novelist when he wrote *Hoot*. This was the first time he'd written a book for young people. He was mostly known for writing environmental thrillers aimed at adults. He wrote *Hoot* partly so his younger relatives would finally be able to read one of his books! The novel is about a boy who moves to Florida and finds himself caught up in the battle to save a rare species of burrowing owls. Hiassen lives in Florida and cares deeply about the environmental issues there. The burrowing owls in the novel are real. Hiassen made them the center of the plot because of how strongly he feels about protecting them.

The main character of both the novel and the film is Roy Eberhardt. Roy is from Montana, but his father's job brings his family to Florida. There he finds himself in a new school, and on the wrong side of a local bully. He also makes friends with a couple of misfits: a girl named Beatrice and her brother, nick-named "Mullet Fingers." Meanwhile, a new pancake house is being constructed in the town—right where the rare burrowing owls live. The trio decides to stand up for the owls against the pancake company's ruthless CEO.

Like Bobby McCallister, Roy Eberhardt presented Logan with the role of a young man who has trouble fitting in. Also like Bobby, Roy learned to stand up for what he believed in. That determination to make a difference is at the heart of the film and Logan's work in it. Talking about the film with TeenHollywood, he said, "I think the main message of this movie in my opinion, is that you can be any age and make a difference. That's what it really teaches you."

Hoot also gave Logan an opportunity to work closely with some other young actors. His friend Dean Collins had a role in the film. He also got the chance to connect with Brie Larson (who plays Beatrice) and Cody Linley (who plays Mullet Fingers). In an interview with the three stars, Cody said, "We had a blast on and off set. . . . We all play guitar so we'd make up this game where you made up a song." Brie continued, "I was, 'okay, you two have to make up a song about me' and the two of them would. . . . Then I had to choose which was the best." The genuine friendship between the teens showed through in their performances on film.

Although the novel *Hoot* had been a Newbery Honor book, the film wasn't well liked by critics. However, Logan's acting still demanded to be recognized. He won his third Young Artist Award for the role, this time for Best Performance in a Feature Film by a leading young actor.

▼ At the time that Logan Lerman's friend Dean Collins was starring with him in the movie Hoot, Dean was also acting in a TV series called The War at Home. Here is Dean (center) with his TV costars Kaylee DeFer (left) and Kyle Sullivan.

Bigger and Better Roles

Over the next few years, Logan continued getting bigger and better roles in film. In his very next project, Logan got the chance to work with one of his favorite actors, the rubber-faced comedian Jim Carrey. He co-stars as Carrey's son in *The Number 23*, a thriller directed by Joel Schumacher. Although Carrey is known for his comedy work, *The Number 23* is a dark, sometimes violent film. It is about a man who becomes obsessed with a mystery novel that he believes is somehow connected to his life.

Logan is a huge fan of Carrey's more serious work, especially his performance in the romantic science fiction film *Eternal Sunshine of the Spotless Mind*. Working with one of the world's most famous stars would be a thrill for anyone. Logan, as always, looked at it as a chance to become a better actor. Talking to the *LA Times* about working with Carrey he said, "I don't know if he would remember this, but he would sit down with me and tell me all about his life, how he got into acting. I also learned a lot from how he prepares for roles. You pick up techniques from other people; you find what works for you. But being able to see how he does it, being able to talk to him, really helped me a lot."

This was far from the last time Logan would work with major stars. His next film put him side by side with two of the most successful and renowned actors in Hollywood. *3:10 to Yuma* is a remake of a classic 1957 Western. Director James Mangold is noted for his skillful craftsmanship on the film. However, it

▲ *Logan Lerman poses with his* The Number 23 *costars. From left to right are: Virginia Madsen, Logan Lerman, Jim Carrey, and Danny Huston.*

was the intense and layered work done by its cast that earned the film the most attention. *3:10 to Yuma* is one of the few remakes of classic films often called better than the original. As famous film critic Roger Ebert said in his review, "Here the quality of the acting, and the thought behind the film, make it seem like . . . something new, even though it's a remake of a good movie 50 years old."

Christian Bale plays Dan Evans, a rancher whose family is struggling to survive. Russell Crowe plays Ben Wade, a notorious outlaw. Evans is given the task of escorting Wade to a train that will take him to prison—the train, of course, is the 3:10 to Yuma. The reward money for the job will save Evans's family. Evans also believes that completing the dangerous task will win him the respect of his son, William. Things get more complicated when William follows them on their journey—and when Wade's old gang comes looking for him.

Logan won the prime role of William, a teenager torn between his love for his decent, hardworking father and his fascination with the strong and charming outlaw, Ben Wade. Logan has always been known for his positivity, and he was typically excited about working so closely with two Hollywood icons. "He's just the coolest guy," he said of Crowe in an interview. He went on to talk about working with Bale. "I'm, like, a huge fan of Christian Bale. I've seen all of his movies. Especially before working with him—I like to study up on who I'm working with, and it's gotta be one of the coolest things to know you can be one of your idols' son[s]."

Perhaps some of Logan's admiration comes from the fact that like Logan, Bale had begun acting at a young age. At just thirteen years old, Bale became a critical favorite for his work in Steven Spielberg's *Empire of the Sun*. He even won a Young Artist Award for the role, just as Logan had for *Hoot*. While some young actors have trouble maintaining careers as they get older, Bale's work includes an Academy Award for *The Fighter* and the starring role in Christopher Nolan's enormously successful Batman films. Like Bale, Logan isn't content to be known only as a good-looking teen star. He told the *LA Times*, "I want to be a good actor more than anything, someone you can respect."

A Heroic Schedule

Both *The Number 23* and *3:10 to Yuma* were released in 2007, and Logan's year wasn't over yet. Later he appeared in the comedy *Meet Bill*, directed by Bernie Goldmann and Melisa Wallack. The film wasn't well received, but Logan's confident work in it proved to be a bright spot for critics.

Juggling acting roles isn't all Logan packed into his schedule as a teenager. On set, he continued his education with a tutor. Between jobs, though, he would return to life as a normal teen going to high

Christian Bale (left) and Russell Crowe (right) are the main stars of 3:10 to Yuma. Logan Lerman plays the son of Christian Bale's character.

school and living with his family. Logan attended Beverly Hills High School. The school is famous, having appeared in a number of films and television shows, including *Clueless* and *90210*. Logan's family was intent that he should finish his education. He graduated high school, but the decision about whether or not to go to college was more difficult. Though his parents were concerned, he eventually decided that college would have to take a backseat to his career. His continued success in finding work helped convince his parents that he was doing the right thing.

Despite his early entry into show business, Logan doesn't feel affected by fame. For the most part, his life was just like any other kid's. He often had a typical school experience, although other times he learned from on-set tutors. Though he doesn't follow sports, he does enjoy playing them. Growing up he was enthusiastic about soccer, baseball, and basketball. Music has also been important to his life. He plays the guitar, among other instruments. He likes both modern indie rock bands like The Strokes and Arcade Fire, as well as classic rock like The Rolling Stones, Neil Young, and Elton John. He also enjoys the work of film composers, including Carter Burwell (who wrote music for films such as *Miller's Crossing, Twilight, The Blind Side*), Michael Giacchino (*The Incredibles, Mission: Impossible III, Star Trek*), and John Williams (*Star Wars, Raiders of the Lost Ark, Harry Potter and the Sorcerer's Stone*).

Like anyone else, Logan also likes to spend time with his friends. Even hanging out, his work is rarely far from his mind, though. Talking about what he does in his spare time, he said, "My friends and I are constantly coming up with situations and plots. We're just gathering ideas constantly, even for fun—they are our conversations, talking about upcoming projects or even just the news, that's what I do with my free time."

With his career, his education, his friends, and his short films keeping him busy, does he have time for a personal life? Logan rarely goes into details about dating—he even claims he still has trouble thinking of himself as a heartthrob. He told RTÉ, "That's the title you get in a poll or in a magazine, but I don't know. In my own life, I'm living at home still; I'm still at my parents' house. I'm 19 so I can't really relate to that situation or that title. I am just kind of reserved and quiet!"

My One and Only and *Gamer*

Logan appeared in two films in 2009. The first was called *My One and Only*, with acclaimed actress Renée Zellweger. Directed by Richard Loncraine, the film centers on the relationship between Anne Devereaux, played by Zellweger, and her son George, played by Logan. The character of George is based on actor George Hamilton. Hamilton was famous as a heartthrob leading man in the 1960s and 1970s. The veteran star couldn't have been happier with Logan's work. He said, "He is very much me. . . . I think he gave a wonderful performance."

▲ Logan Lerman (left) is pictured with two other stars of *My One and Only*, *Reneé Zellweger and Mark Randall.*

Gamer is a sci-fi thriller in which rich teenagers play video games with real people trapped as the characters in the games. Gerard Butler plays a convicted murderer named Kable fighting for his freedom, and Logan Lerman plays his player, Simon. This was a new type of role for Logan—he portrays a character who is crude, insensitive, and kills people by controlling Kable in the video game. While he slipped into the role of a spoiled rich kid with a nasty streak easily enough, the film failed. *Gamer*'s lack of success hasn't held Logan back, though. His most memorable role was still to come.

5 Percy Jackson and Beyond

One night years ago, a boy named Haley Riordan asked his father to read him a bedtime story. Rick Riordan was a teacher and writer, and so storytelling came naturally to him. Haley had recently been diagnosed with attention deficit hyperactivity disorder (ADHD), a disorder that makes it difficult to concentrate, and dyslexia, a disorder that makes it hard to read. Both these conditions can make life difficult for a kid at school, and Riordan was happy to tell any story to help his son feel better. Haley didn't just want any story, though—he wanted a story about the heroes from Greek mythology. Riordan eagerly told his son all the mythical tales he knew.

Ancient Greek mythology tells about the Olympians. The Olympians are gods and goddesses that ruled the world from the top of Mount Olympus. Zeus was the king of the gods and the master of the sky. His brothers were Poseidon, god of the sea, and Hades, god of the underworld. The queen of the gods was Zeus's wife, Hera, and together they had many children who were also gods. Zeus even had some children that were partly human—demigods. Demigods were mortal like other

▲ Rick Riordan, author of the series of books featuring Percy Jackson, signs books for fans.

men and women, but had inherited special abilities from an immortal parent. The demigods were often heroes. The Greeks told stories of the powerful Heracles (better known as Hercules), the nearly invincible Achilles, and the beautiful Helen of Troy.

But when Rick Riordan had told his son all the stories he knew, Haley still wanted to hear more. That was when Riordan decided to make up his own hero. This hero was a demigod like many of the heroes in Greek mythology, but one who lived in modern-day America. He even gave the character ADHD and dyslexia and a host of problems with school. Riordan called his new hero Percy Jackson. Haley liked Percy's story so much he encouraged his dad to write it all down in a book. This book became *The Lightning Thief*, the first in Riordan's best-selling series of books about modern-day demigods, or "half-bloods."

The Olympians Take Manhattan

In *The Lightning Thief*, Percy is a troublesome middle-school kid who never knew his father. After one of his teachers, the nasty Mrs. Dodds, tries to kill him, Percy discovers that his life isn't what he thought it was. His ADHD and dyslexia aren't just conditions that make his life tougher; they're signs that he's descended from one of the Olympian gods. The father he never knew is actually Poseidon, the sea god. His best friend, Grover, is a faun. A faun is a mythical creature that lives in the forest and has the legs and horns of a goat. Grover has been sent to watch over Percy in case any monsters try to hurt him—monsters like Mrs. Dodds. Mrs. Dodds was really one of the vicious furies—winged creatures the gods use to punish their enemies. He's soon taken to a place called Camp Half-Blood, where people like him are trained to be heroes and protect themselves from the monsters.

At Camp Half-Blood, Percy learns that the Greek gods are no longer in Greece. The gods have been a force moving and changing along with Western civilization. In the modern day, they no longer rule from a mountaintop in Greece. Instead, the entrance to the home of the gods is atop the Empire State Building in Manhattan. But this new home for Olympus isn't safe. Someone has stolen Zeus's ultimate weapon—his lightning bolt. Percy is given a quest. He, his friend Grover, and another half-blood named Annabeth must try to find the bolt and figure out who stole it. If they don't complete this quest in time, it could cause a war between the gods that will tear the world apart.

The Lightning Thief was released in 2005, and in just two years it had already sold more than 250,000 copies. Its sequel, *The Sea of Monsters*, sold an additional 100,000. With a third book in the immensely popular series on the way, it was only natural that Hollywood would be interested in Percy's story. In 2007, director Chris Columbus decided to write and direct an adaptation to be called *Percy Jackson and the Olympians: The Lightning Thief*.

Putting Percy on Film

Few people have as much experience making movies for young people as Chris Columbus. From his first feature, 1987's *Adventures in Babysitting*, he's specialized in telling stories about kids—especially kids thrust into scary situations. His credits include the Macaulay Culkin films *Home Alone* and *Home Alone 2: Lost in New York*, in which a young boy uses ingenious traps to battle a pair of dim-witted thieves.

Columbus may be most famous, however, for helping to adapt the sensational Harry Potter series to the big screen by directing *Harry Potter and the Sorcerer's Stone* and *Harry Potter and the Chamber of Secrets*. With these colossal successes under his belt, he turned his sights on Percy Jackson. But to do the character justice, he'd need the right actor.

▼ *Logan Lerman and some of the cast of* Percy Jackson and the Olympians: The Lightning Thief *visit the top of the Empire State Building, which is featured in the film. From left to right are: Pierce Brosnan, Kevin McKidd, Alexandra Daddario, Brandon T. Jackson, and Logan Lerman.*

Luckily for Logan, Columbus was already a fan. He'd seen Logan's performance in *3:10 to Yuma*, and he'd been impressed. In an interview about the film, he said, ". . . I was completely taken by this kid. I thought that was a pretty good performance for a 14-year-old and I kept him in the back of my head. So when we were casting Percy, I asked Logan to come into the office and read and then we did the screen test and I have to say I was very impressed." With Columbus behind him, Logan easily won the part.

That's where the easy part ended—now Logan needed to transform from a normal teenager into a demigod. While Logan enjoys sports, his passions have always been film and music—so when it came to getting into the physical aspects of the movie, he had some work to do. For combat scenes, he did sword training and martial arts. To do scenes with Percy's flying shoes, he had to work with five different rigs to keep him in the air on set. He even had to learn how to scuba dive for scenes set underwater! Fortunately, he was already a good swimmer—it would've been a little embarrassing to see the son of a sea god doing a doggie paddle.

Logan also needed to get to know his new co-stars. Percy's friend and fellow half-blood Annabeth was played by Alexandra Daddario, while the role of Grover went to Brandon T. Jackson. Each of them brought something special to his or her role. Columbus was struck by Alexandra's eyes. He saw an otherworldly quality in them that made him believe she could be the daughter of Athena. Jackson had impressed Columbus

▲ *From left to right, the three young stars of* Percy Jackson and the Olympians: The Lightning Thief: *Brandon T. Jackson, Alexandra Daddario, and Logan Lerman.*

with his gift for humor in the film *Tropic Thunder*. What they both had in common was chemistry with Logan. The three young actors would be spending a lot of time on film together, and the most important thing was making audiences believe that they liked and cared about each other. Of course, this wasn't all acting. According to Logan, "We were spending every day together, so that we could have that natural chemistry on a screen, so we all ended up becoming close friends. We all would hang out all the time, off set. We were a little family."

Logan's relationship with Alexandra was especially important,

because not only did they have to be friends, but they also had to be rivals. In fact, they even had to face each other in a sword fight! Filming the battle was a new experience for Logan. He'd never been in combat against another actor before. The two young stars were reluctant to hit

◀ *Logan Lerman and Alexandra Daddario had to have great chemistry because they acted in so many scenes together in the first Percy Jackson film.*

each other the way they would a stunt performer who'd been trained for years to do combat scenes. Logan eventually came up with a way to convince Alexandra to put some force into the fight—he lied to her. He told her that he was wearing padding, and that she could hit him or kick him and he'd be fine. Of course, he wasn't wearing padding at all! Logan was pleased with the results. "It really added to that realistic quality of the scene because she was actually beating me up," he said in one interview, laughing.

The chemistry between the two actors was actually so good that some fans suspected there was more than friendship to their off-screen relationship. After filming, though, *USA Today* asked Logan if he had a girlfriend. "No. I'm single," he replied. When pressed whether he thought that fact might be of interest to his fans, he said he had no idea, but added, "I hope so."

Beyond Percy Jackson

Although *The Lightning Thief* didn't have the same box-office punch as Columbus's work on the Harry Potter series, the film grossed more than $225 million worldwide. Many critics felt like the work was too similar to the Potter films. *Entertainment Weekly* said, it had "all the CGI sorcery of a Harry Potter pic, but none of the magic." However, other critics disagreed. The film received a lot of praise for its ability to make Greek myths fun. The *Newark Star-Ledger*'s review said, "With great effects (and a few surprises) it's a fun, Saturday-matinee adventure."

It was successful enough that pre-production has begun on a sequel based on Riordan's second Percy Jackson novel, *The Sea of Monsters*.

Logan isn't content to just be known as Percy Jackson, though. Shortly after his work on *The Lightning Thief*, he signed up to play another young hero from literature—D'Artagnan, from Alexandre Dumas's classic novel *The Three Musketeers*. Director Paul W. S. Anderson adapted the French novel about three legendary swordsmen who unite with a young warrior to save the royal family of France. Logan's experience as Percy Jackson helped him lock down the role without the audition process he'd been used to on his previous films. Perhaps Anderson was impressed not only by his talent, but also by his experience with a sword—anyone playing D'Artagnan has to be able to fence. Logan had to spend hours in the gym every day for months to learn all the complex screen combat. The role was also a chance for Logan to play a different kind of character—one who was cocky and impulsive enough to make the heroic Percy Jackson look meek in comparison. "I think he's the most different character to me that I've ever played," he said of the role.

Logan's next film put him back in a more familiar situation— that of a misfit trying to belong. In writer and director Stephen Chbosky's *The Perks of Being a Wallflower*, Logan puts down the swords to be part of a quieter story. He plays Charlie, a freshman in high school who's shy and troubled. Charlie begins to open up after meeting two seniors who try to help

Logan Lerman attends the premiere of The Three Musketeers.

◀ *Logan Lerman promotes* The Three Musketeers *in Japan.*

him adjust to high school. The film also features another young star of fantasy family films—Emma Watson, famous for her role as Hermione in the Harry Potter films. For all Logan's success, he had never had the same level of attention that Watson received for that role, and he was fascinated by it. Of course, in his typical positive fashion, he had nothing but good things to say about his co-star. "... she is an incredibly bright and talented person and handles it very well," he said.

After *The Perks of Being a Wallflower*, Logan has two independent films lined up. The first is *Stuck in Love*, a comedy/drama written and directed by Josh Boone. Logan will be co-starring with Greg Kinnear, Jennifer Connelly, and Lily Collins. The four actors will play a broken family with a complex set of relationships. The second indie film is *The Only Living Boy in New York*. A different set of complex relationships crops up in this film. Logan stars as a boy who discovers his father is having an affair with a younger woman.

Fans of Logan's work as a swashbuckling action star don't have to worry—it's unlikely he'll stay away from the heroic roles for long. The next Percy Jackson film is planned for release in 2013. Lerman will also be in the epic film *Noah* (2014) with his *3:10 to Yuma* costar Russell Crowe.

Logan has found so much success playing unlikely heroes—from a nerdy misfit who'll one day be president of the United States to a troubled teenager who discovers that he's the son of a god—that it's hard to imagine he won't return to them throughout his career. The challenge for Logan will be growing up on-screen.

Many young actors have had trouble maintaining their careers as they become adults. Today, Logan has graduated from high school and made the decision to focus on his career. Although he still lives with his family, his life and his career are entering a new stage. Logan seems to look forward to the change, though. Talking about how his career is developing, he said, "... [A]s you get older, there are different types of roles and different points in people's lives ... it's interesting to tackle those things on

◀ *Logan Lerman has a more grown-up look for his movie* The Perks of Being a Wallflower.

screen as I'm living them. ... [It's having] to keep it honest; living an honest life."

Hollywood seems to agree. Logan's career has only seemed to gain steam as he's grown up. His *The Lightning Thief* director, Chris Columbus, certainly predicts great things for Logan's future. "I think Percy Jackson is just the beginning for him," he said. "He's a teenager with the mindset of a 60-year-old. He's committed, he's so intelligent and I don't think he's concerned with fame or any of that nonsense. He's concerned about creating really strong movies."

Further Info

Books

Knight, Mary-Jane, *Percy Jackson and the Olympians: The Ultimate Guide.* New York: Hyperion, 2010.

Riordan, Rick, *The Demigod Files (A Percy Jackson and the Olympians Guide).* New York: Hyperion, 2009.

Riordan, Rick and Wilson, Leah, *Demigods and Monsters: Your Favorite Authors on Rick Riordan's Percy Jackson and the Olympians Series.* Dallas, TX: BenBella Books, Inc., 2009.

Internet Addresses

Logan Lerman's official Web site
 <http://loganlerman.com>

Rick Riordan's official website

Jack and Bobby online
 <http://www.thewb.com/shows/jack-and-bobby>

Index